GRUNDEN

GRUNDEN

A
Poetry Anthology

James C. Spangenberg

Library of Congress Control Number:		2019906783
ISBN:	Hardcover	978-1-7960-3834-7
	Softcover	978-1-7960-3833-0
	eBook	978-1-7960-3832-3

Print information available on the last page.

Rev. date: 06/13/2019

To order additional copies of this book, contact:
Xlibris
1-888-795-4274
www.Xlibris.com
Orders@Xlibris.com
796227

To My Wife,

Wendy,

As simply as I can say,

Thank you for all the support and love

A&F

James

Foreword

Grunden; *found (German Translation)*

Found; *(adj.) the past and post participle of find, having been*

discovered unexpectedly

to establish or set up, especially with the

provision for continuing existence

The evolution of our being begins with no expectations, no limitations, and no prejudice. Along the rather fragile journey we call life, it is quickly discovered that there are unlimited factors that impede our path to what we think of as our destiny. The milestones which are either bestowed or achieved throughout the "journey of life," ultimately determine our destination. Where you finally end up is defined and determined by you and you alone. Many factors along the path we take will outline our goals and how we achieve them. This anthology outlines and highlights some of those in its sectors. Hopefully the entries will summon reflection and insight into your thought process and allow you to follow along on the journey to a place where you too can be Grunden.

<u>STRIFE</u>

Strife; *(noun) defined as an angry or bitter disagreement/*
conflict over fundamental issues; the conflict an act of contention,
fight or struggle, physical or non-physical in nature

Strife *as it is defined in a biblical sense, is a vigorous or bitter conflict with*
someone else. It can be a struggle or clash with another person that may include
violence or even armed conflict. Strife can sometimes include violent disagreements
within a group as well as with those in positions of authority. Strife has found
its way and been called out in the ancient scriptures from Genesis to Proverbs.
Solomon, in his great wisdom, wrote about the source of strife in Proverbs 10:12,
"Hatred stirs up strife, but love covers all offenses." Because "by insolence comes
nothing but their emotions, this is easy to comprehend.

Strife *will find its way into all of our lives. How we overcome it is*
paramount to how we, as civilized people, settle our differences and come
together as one, harmonic society. Anything short of that equates to civil discord
and even war. Great battles were avoided by Abraham's ability to mitigate the
strife between the shepherds of his flocks. Where the herds would graze became

a tumultuous debate and lent itself to near physical encounters. Only calming and sensible drafting of words eliminated the strife between the herdsmen.

Strife can besiege the minds and bodies of a great many. As you digest the entries in Sector I, the message of strife that surrounds us every day, hopefully, is evident. The darkest hours of any human being cannot be defined nor felt by another. How we manage those feelings and whether we stay in or out of control determines the level of corruption within our soul.

Strife, if great enough, can lend no recourse to change the inevitable nor mitigate the demise of humanity. It will remain with us and will continue to corrupt the body, minds, and souls of all until time ceases to exist.

SECTOR I

STRIFE

- *Spirit Thief*
- *Alien*
- *Epidemic*
- *Liquid Demon*
- *Addict*
- *Stolen*
- *Fade to Dark*

This sector is a journey to the darker side of human thought and the personal struggles that can be encountered on the "journey of life." From those thoughts, often times, actions are engaged that have a provocative impact on the outcome of our personal and social being. Everyone has them but to what extent they are scripted and or acted out within the daily life determines the ultimate impact they have on our existence.

Spirit Thief

An eerie moon creeps across the sky

The spirit world is restless

The wounded wolf begins his cry

For the mating of the temptress

With nails of crimson and fangs of white

She hunts all alone for her prey

Her goal to take a soul tonight

Must finish before dawn of day

An old man walks a deserted trail

A young boy is by his side

Both will fight to no avail

The thirsty vixen must fill her pride

The wind blows bloody across the lawn

A gruesome portrait is cast

Both man and child so quickly gone

They will not be the last

Alien

A street lamp glows in the dark of night

Lonesome shadows are all around

A man stands smoking, embers burn bright

Careless, he tosses remains to the ground

Two young women walk alone on the street

No questions as to what's on their mind

Unlike the bum, they're not looking to eat

It's money they want, it's money they'll find

A baby cries and a woman screams

The night air is filled with fear

Two more souls losing out on a dream

What kind of people live in places like this

Who are they and where are they from

Are they choosing to stay merely to exist

Or could it be worse from where they've come

Epidemic

Can anyone but me hear the crying

As the children lay hungry in bed

All around them the screams of the dying

And the stench of those already dead

Mothers stand helpless, bankrupt of hope

No one from this place can live

A missionary urges the healthy to cope

But words are all he can give

There is no solution to this impossible task

No way to achieve any goal

Purgatory beckons, its leader in a mask

Ultimately loving them out of their souls

People keep coming no matter who leaves

They've not tried to put this to an end

With a devil masquerading as a friend

Liquid Demon

I fight the devil that shakes my hands

He's made me weak and made me old

He'll be here at day's start and end

Be here rain, sunshine, or cold

This demon sits, patience of steel

Waiting for me to start the fight

Although not bloody, the wounds are real

Victory is nowhere in sight

This enemy of mine has many faces

Brown, white, or gold who knows

His crimson sword is as sharp as any

Once touched it, like fungus, grows

The viscous scars upon this heart

Only healed after he departs

Or death will be his victory

Addict

Nothing I can tell you

Can make you change your mind

Years of non-conformity

Have ultimately sealed your fate

No matter where you go in life

You will always be the same

Unbending, unforgiving, unpleasant

It's not your fault that you are made this way

It's simply a chemical factor

Your body no longer listens to your mind

Your mind no longer listens to you

The preaching is over

What's done is done

There's only praying left to do

And even that may be futile

For it seems the years of destruction

Have found their way into

Your soul

Stolen

I feel the steel upon my flesh

Warm blood begins to flow

I stand alone in quiet distress

No time to run, no place to go

I did not see the culprit's face

He hides behind a mask

Fleeing as if he's in a race

To stop the dying, my only task

I hope the bounty does some good

Helps the homeless or those in need

I'd have given freely if I could

Rather than stand alone and bleed

But God will guide his soul and mine

And someday we two will meet

Then he and I can spend some time

Without fear, each other greet

Fade to Dark

There are no perfect days for me

The nights are long and cold

Evil roams my body freely

There is nothing left to hold

Except the notion that there's life beyond

What I've worked so hard to gain

Affords me little comfort

The finality does not eclipse the pain

With all that should be done

It is there each waking day

Everyone around me proclaims

Just go along your merry way

Evil has made the path unclear

I've not worshipped like I should

Dark days draw nearer

Times becoming sad

I hope the end even though be long

Will allow some sort of comfort

EMOTIONS

Emotions; *e-mo-tions (plural noun)*

a natural instinctive state of mind deriving from one's

circumstances, mood, or relationships with others;

instinctive or intuitive feeling as distinguished from reason or knowledge

Emotions *are defined by three elements: cognitive, behavioral, and physiological. Some emotions are outwardly noticeable. Excitement, for example, can be evident by shaking hands or a trembling body. It can transpire into something as subtle as a quiver in the voice. Regardless how openly noticeable, the effect of the emotion on the physical body is self-explanatory.*

Emotions *drive deep, inner, feelings that can inhibit the way we think and act. Sometimes the strongest emotions lay quiet. The heavy pulse of an exposed neck vein may be the only evidence that exists in an otherwise stoic body. The emotion causing that reaction may be quite intense. Those feelings can and do alter the cognitive thought process. Thoughts and actions that allow us to live and exist are governed by the laws of the land, nature, and God. That cognitive process that takes us to where we can ultimately live is fueled by the raw emotion to stay alive, to exist.*

Emotions that exist deep within oneself provoke cognitive, behavioral, and physiological responses. Often those go unnoticed or unrecognized as exceptional. The first, gentle touch of a newborn son by his father's patiently waiting hand can stir an unmeasurable response. Although it may be clearly guarded and controlled, raw emotion can rise above the normal realm of behavior and show itself in an unchanneled physical response, even violent reactions that would not normally be predictable.

Emotions have been the catalyst for the choices selected for Sector II. A myriad of feelings, profound thoughts, and emotions have sculpted the writing that the author hopes will stir you.

SECTOR II

EMOTIONS

- *Depression*

- *Quiet Anguish*

- *Somewhere*

- *Ponder Demise*

- *Life Puzzle*

- *Always with Me*

- *Place*

This sectors selection outline where Emotions can take you. The thoughts and feelings within, mirror where you have been in Sector I. There is a great irony in how certain emotions lend themselves to responses and destinations in which one chooses to reside.

Depression

The rain falls sideways

Today of all days

The gloom is an unwelcomed

Visitor

So many days will be

Dark and void

I could scream but

No one would hear

I will wait impatiently

For tomorrow

Hopefully that day is different

Sunshine and blue skies

Might make the pain go away

If only for a short time

But if it rains and the sky is black

I will surely try and

Remember

To make it through until the next day

The sun shines once again

Quiet Anguish

Can I tell her that I'm terrified?

Is it selfish to be afraid?

Does she know I stayed awake and cried

God take this pain away

There are no answers, just the wait

What's more painful I don't know

I need to talk, but now it's late

This can wait until tomorrow

It may be nothing, just a false alarm

No need to worry like this now

As she lies there sleeping, I touch her arm

Wondering if I'll cope and how

Faith encourages us to be strong

I pray the Almighty can see

What touches so many, seems so wrong

I curse this damn disease

Somewhere

Somewhere a flower blossoms

Somewhere it snows or rains

Tonight another child forgotten

More turmoil and more pain

Somewhere a man weeps all alone

His belly hurts from hunger

So many people with no home

The killers getting younger

Somewhere life taken for a bag of dope

A car stolen because it's there

The faithful quickly losing hope

A society that no longer cares

We need to change the way we live

We must learn again to care

Before there's nothing left to give

We need to find somewhere

Ponder Demise

Sometimes I sit and wonder

How this all will end

Will I hear a clap of thunder

Or the calling of a friend

I hope that I see sunshine

Each day I'm here on earth

But even in the darkest times

I am thankful for my birth

With help of faith, I hold true

My hopes, my dreams, my fears

And understand what I've been through

In the passing of the years

Every day with you brings sunshine

Even though there's clouds and rain

It's that moment when your eyes meet mine

I no longer feel the pain

Life Puzzle

There is no journey without destination

There's no end without a start

No problem exists without a solution

No compassion where there's no heart

There can be no river without a stream

No mountains unless there are stones

Reality pointless if there is no dream

Only a house if there isn't a home

Is there vision if you have no eyes

Can there be sound if you have no ears

Do clouds exist without a sky

Are there worries if there is no fear

Pieces of life depend on each other

The way they're molded determines our fate

Existence begins with the father and mother

Life begins at almighty's gate

Always with Me

When all todays become the past

And the years remove the sorrow

The pain you thought would always last

Is masked by new tomorrows

There is no way to ever soften

The mighty blow dealt on that day

I look to heaven and think of her often

Still sad she was taken away

I still see her face and that smile she had

I talk to her picture every now and then

I remember her laugh and how she never got mad

How she always helped no matter who or when

I hope when my time on this earth ends

I'll have passage to a place where I'll see

A wife and mother and everyone's friend

But to me, always, Grandma Marie

A Place

The loneliest thing that I know

Isn't that far away

It doesn't breathe and doesn't grow

And can't tell night from day

There are no windows from which to see

What's going on outside

You can exist but cannot be

You can seek but cannot hide

The wind never blows in this place

There are no streams full of fish

There is a life, but it has no face

There are no thoughts, there's just a wish

If you don't find it, let it go

It's the only place you'll ever need

And when it's touched you will surely know

Break it and it will bleed

***Hope;** (noun)*

a feeling of expectation and desire for a certain thin to happen

a feeling of trust

__Hope__ is an objective state of mind that is based on the expectation of positive outcomes within someone's life. It has long been conveyed that hope can lead the masses and conquer all beasts. Without it, we as a civilization become complacent and lethargic in action and word. Throughout history hope has been the catalyst to peace and serenity between nations who otherwise would have destroyed one another.

__Hope__ has also been well- documented within the scriptures and other great writings of the world. One of the most profound examples of hope championing the masses was documented and re-told in the scriptures. Passed down through the ages, this incredible story of hope continues to influence millions of people around the world. Moses stood high on the mount and proclaimed the word of God Almighty to the masses below him who had lost all faith. Hope and promise brought them out of the darkness of Egypt and the bondage that had harnessed them for generations.

***Hope** in our lifetime has been disguised by many faces. People pin their dreams on words and contracts from corporations and governments. Each entity promises some sort of gain or positive outcome if we remain hopeful.*

***Hope**, and what is gained by having it, has somehow gotten lost within certain factors of our society. Some of the travesties are called out in Sector I and II. Hope can awaken even the darkest spirits among us and only an open mind and thoughtful relevance to a significant outcome is needed. Hopefully this sector will allow you to glance into what our journey is and where it will ultimately end.*

SECTOR III

HOPE

- *Lonely Walking*
- *Lily*
- *Tree*
- *A Storm*
- *Pathways*
- *Runaway*
- *Daddy's Girl*

This sector depicts a brighter side of where our emotions can take us. The world around us is comprised of unique individuals who live and exist on a premise of a better world and a better life for themselves and for those around them. The selections within are depictions of what the author envisions as the roadmap to hope.

Lonely Walking

Yesterday I took a lonely walk

I saw people everywhere

No one looked, no one would talk

It seemed they did not care

Care to listen, or take the time

To try and make a friend

In the park I stood and watched a mime

And learned as much from him

How can we live entombed like this

A society without a face

Where life goes by with so much missed

And at such a frantic pace

So on my lonely walk today

I vowed to end this sorrow

I'll help just one along the way

And do the same again tomorrow

Lily

Today I looked into small bright eyes

Happy just to see I'm home

A mountain of doubt awaits the child

No fault of anyone here, just bad luck

We can only love and care for her

Put our deepest prejudice aside

Hope and pray she'll know no pain

And comfort her if she does

There is no formula for exactly why

Some creatures abandon their young

The convenience of a liberal society

Has surely contributed to it

To make sense or reason for all unknowns

Takes a wisdom far greater than mine

My only hope is that someday

For an instant she understands

Tree

A seedling sprouts from in the ground

It's birth unrecognized

No father, mother, can be found

All alone it must survive

It battles summer's long, hot draught

Stands fast in cold of winter

Springtime rains bring its buds out

Summer lightning leaves it splintered

A few small seeds fall to the floor

Of a forest charred and grey

A fresh new rain has come once more

A new tree is born today

A carpenter will sit and wait

For the tree to grow strong and tall

He'll use the lumber for heaven's gate

Storm

Sometime stand in the pouring rain

And listen to the thunder

It seems to take away the pain

But also makes me wonder

What

So powerful and so dangerous

Delivered by God's awesome might

Is a cleansing that he gives to us

Eerie spectacle yet awesome sight

Yet

Sometimes the anger of the storm

Gives no reason nor sheds a light

Why such destruction seen in the morn'

Like a thief came in the night

But as we look and wonder why

Things slowly begin to mend

The daughnting black goes to blue sky

It's time to help a friend

Pathways

In the bright and clear new light of day

It's now so easy to see

We have no trouble finding our way

We know just where to be

But then as always darkness breaks

And the path gets hard to find

The creatures of the night awake

Those of the day turn blind

By God's design we're not of the night

But look up and you will see

The splendor of the northern lights

And hear how quiet the night can be

This new day will bring sunshine

That will warm the soul within

Finding you way might take some time

With God's help you can begin

Runaway

A bird of prey can only fly

With killing on its mind

It has no choice, you wonder why

Life hangs on every find

If you could fly, what would you be

A songbird or a hawk

To sit and sing from a tree

Or be forever on the stalk

Failures come, and failures go

They're there with every tide

To choose to run and never know

A safe place you can hide

So fly back home if you choose

The game of life you must not lose

Spread your wings and grow

Daddy's Girl

This morning I sat in the naughty chair

I truly don't know why

Too bad about my brother's hair

I didn't mean to make him cry

Mommy said just wait for dad

He'll know what to do

Don't even think that I was bad

Who'd know don't mix with glue hair

I hear my brother holler

As Mommy cuts and snips

Tight hug around my daddy's collar

Little legs wrapped around his hips

I really, really love you dad

I don't know where Mommy is

But Daddy she seems really mad

How bout' a great big kiss

DESTINATION

Destination; *des-ti-na-tion: (noun)*

the place to which someone or something is going or being sent: (adj) being a place that people will make a special trip or visit the ultimate purpose for which something is created or intended the predetermined end of a journey or voyage; the ultimate end

*A **Destination** is and can be fraught with pitfalls and obstacles. Early on your journey you must have some idea or pre-determined endpoint. How we arrive there and ultimately how peaceful that journey is will be determined by factors and feelings that are outlined in the writings of Sector IV.*

The destination will be considered complete if along the way someone else recognizes the journey's importance. The author hopes that the choices within will help you identify what your journey is and ultimately reach your own **Destination***.*

SECTOR IV

DESTINATION

- *Spring Awakens*

- *Mother Earth*

- *Island Dream*

- *The Pond*

- *Time*

- *Quest*

Everyone has a different idea or concept of what a destination is. When asked, most people will tell you that they begin at one point and end up at what they consider their destination. In this sector we choose to look at destination in a more conceptual way. Not only physical places, but somewhere in our minds can be the ultimate end to a journey.

Spring Awakens

A frosty halo surrounds the moon

Like a mask upon a face

Winters grip will be gone soon

And spring will take its place

Night winds blow, not quite so cold

The sun warmer each new day

A river runs brown and bold

Gathering strength along the way

The skunk and bear rise from their nap

Awakened by spring hunger

An old man works on trees to tap

Teaching grandson, decades younger

All the seasons come and go

Each different but the same

One thing certain that the elder knows

With spring will come the rain

Mother Earth

The land can give back

Only what it receives

If slighted, the seas become angry

You can hear the displeasure on the wind

You can smell disappointment in the air

The beasts of the land become unruly

Threatened by all the destruction

They seem to understand

What the ancient elders have taught

They appear ready to defend it

The circle of life begins here

It must be coddled and nurtured

To remain we must certainly understand

It will not be created

Again

Island Dream

Lying in the dark

I am captivated by the sound

Of waves tumbling into shells and sand

The room has surrendered to fragrant sea air

What is around me is all that exists

No lights dot the beautiful shoreline

Protecting an ancient traveler

On a mission to procreate

The stars and moon are all you see

The vision chiseled into your mind

As beautiful as this place is now

You can only imagine what it was

When all that touched the clean, white sands

Were the moon beams at night

And rays of sunshine every day

The Pond

Many things thrive at the pond

The frogs, the birds, the deer

It's like you wave a magic wand

And living things appear

They bathe in quiet, cool water

Nest on the grassy shores

We swim with sons and daughters

From its dark depths life pours

A small boy swims with great delight

The cool, clear water gleams

The moon reflects off it at night

As the same boy lies and dreams

If everyone could have a pond and

We'd be a happier lot

To sit and watch take me beyond

What Mother Nature has not forgot

Time

Time is merely a concept

It's an invented state of mind

But time is something quite well kept

And what most seem hard to find

There are those certain places

Where time has no meaning

The look on dead and war torn faces

Where life's blood is left streaming

They say that time should not be wasted

That it's precious here on earth

Like fine wine should be savored not tasted

Like gold the beauty as much the worth

It's said in time all wounds will heal

It does not matter how jagged or deep

Thank God the concept is real

Only my soul and time can He keep

Quest

Depart in darkness, find a tree

One on which you'll lean

With back against and gun on sleeve

And pray that you're not seen

First ray of sun, a crow calls out

He sings the woods awake

You hear the gobbler, there's no doubt

Your knees begin to shake

With all your skill you strike the slate

Talking to a master that is so wise

Everyday he's early, but now he is late

In the morning mist you strain your eyes

Like a thief at night he arrives

Full strut in front of you

Carefully you move and take your aim

In a flash the season's through

LIVING

Living; (adj) liv-ing

having life

exhibiting the life or motion of nature

(noun) the condition of being alive means of subsistence

Conduct or manner of life

Living is a concept which has different meanings to many people. For most, the simplest form of life and making their way through it does not constitute living. Living has been defined and used in diction since the early 12th century. It amazes great minds and forward thinkers to this day how people confuse living with being alive.

Everyone has their own, unique way to come to grips with the concept of living and with dying. In Sector V, the selections outline what living means both consciously and unconsciously to the author. The hope is that within all of these selections, the living can continue or begin. That somehow the journey of living will allow you to be grunden.

SECTOR V

LIVING

- *Hunter*

- *Royal Game*

- *Spirit of the Hunter*

- *Where to Live*

- *A Brave Dream*

- *Heaven*

- *City Lost*

Existing in today's world presents many of us with challenges and choices that cannot and should not be taken lightly. Throughout the ages, people have adapted to changing environments and cultural expectations. Each of us has to determine how we choose to live our life and exist in an ever- changing and demanding world. This sectors selections reach into a more spiritual analogy of existence. Everyone can make their own conclusion as to what living really is.

Hunter

The mystery of the beast draws the man

Like a moth to a dancing flame

Primal instincts held, deep within

Nurture and protect the ancient game

A game of skill, mostly one-sided

They hold all the aces

The hunter- gatherer can't be misguided

He must seek his favorite places

To hunt the prey, we must know

Everywhere it chooses to hide

When final lifeblood begins to flow

Rejoice the trophy, for the animal cry

But it will feed my body and soul

I praise the sustenance it gives

To embrace the wild, my only goal

Thankful the wild is where I live

Royal Game

A coachman rides upon the breeze

Guided by a maiden hair

The master's ready, he waits to see

What lurks in the watery lair

The oceans greatness cannot match

What make the master shiver

The lure of the catch and hatch

The mystery of the river

He watches as the coachman lands

Precisely where he's aimed

With the whip held tightly in his hand

He'll play the ancient game

A game of patience, style and grace

Trophies held between the pages

Of minds that know that special place

Passed down throughout the ages

Spirit of the Hunter

*This poem is dedicated to the precious souls lost in an unexplainable act of
violence during a time of sacred family tradition*

I stand among the trees and flowers

And watch the world go by

Sometimes for long and lonely hours

There are those who question why

The answer is a simple one

For myself and for my friends

It's for tradition that it's done

We'll be hunter to the end

Today I gaze upon a quiet lake

The sun shimmers on its shore

The time has come when God must take

Us home to heaven's door

We enter in, the camp light glows

Fathers, daughters, sons, and friends

We need our closest all to know

We're still hunters in the end

Where to Live

There are people who love the bright lights

The noise and crowds of the town

There is music and temptation

On every corner

The smells of countries mingle

No one seems to know each other

Even together they seem alone

It's just on the border of chaos

There's a place that's noisy quiet

The fox and the shrew move together

Across the moonlit terrace

Where it's peaceful and serene

Look around at all that is clean and good

And then at the other side

Pick one or both

It's your choice

Time divided well spent

A Brave Dream

The ancient thunder of their drums

Still echoes through the canyons

Telling stories of young and old

Of greater days lost forever

Days of feasts and many buffalo

When sun and wind ruled the land

Days when honor went unchallenged

And men spoke only the truth

Times when land was left as found

When eagles soared above

The elk and bear lived together

The raven watched from afar

All these things brought together

The land, the water, the air

The wolf and fox still here to roam

Just not as freely now

Heaven

A misty light shines from the woods

Welcoming one and all

No man ever turned away

No child will sleep hungry

Sit and rest your weary eyes

Be warm and try to sleep

A peaceful presence guards the door

A minstrel plays a quiet song

The whippoorwill is telling stories

The moon shines clear and bright

The loon and owl are noisy sentries

Whether real or just a vision

Ancient souls roam fertile soil

Peace remains all through the day

For all the time that's been spent waiting

Once you're here you'll never

Leave

City Lost

What lies beneath the twisted rubble

What secrets yearn to breathe

Years of corruption, hate, and greed

Now covered but not quite gone

Slowly things return to "normal"

If such a thing can be

A calamity of errors to overcome

So many to blame, so few that understand

Artifacts and possessions lost

Like the dead will not return

Hope vanishes at an alarming rate

Some choose to leave forever

If such an event was planned by generals

The script would not be different

To kill them only takes a moment

Take their spirit and you take their life

SECTOR VI

FOUR L'S

(Living, Love, Life, and Laments)

- ***Garden Royalty***

- ***Just for You***

- ***Together Still***

- ***Gin-Mill***

- ***Commander***

- ***Memorial Day***

This final sector is a compilation of thoughts that at one point or other, crossed the mind of the author. Thee are no steadfast rules or significant purpose to the message. At the end of the day, everyone has a place in their mind where they go to archive the outcomes of the actions and events that occurred in a given time period. Each conversation or task is unique in some way, shape, or form.

The events of life tend to find common ground regardless which group you dissect. If you look deep into your own thoughts, you can find some place that is either dark and gloomy or light and uplifting. How we process the emotions that come to the forefront of our actions defines us as a person and tells us who we really and truly are. There are no secret codes or magic potions that trigger the way we think and how we adapt those thoughts to our daily lives. Environment, culture, education, and other outside forces determine that. The mere idea that we alone control how we think and how we act is misguided to say the least.

Our thoughts and actions, although our own, are molded by what surrounds us and how we choose to define and use them. It is what makes us unique. So as we step through this thing called life, we should understand there will be good days and there will be bad. Take each as it comes and digest the meaning of it as it pertains to your course of fate. If you choose correctly, the path will be easy and filled with pleasure and satisfaction. Choose incorrectly and you may regret each day.

Garden Royalty

An intriguing odor comes from the vines

A scent of Kings and Queens

I seek the source in the leafy jungle

And find the pretty bells

Their essence is heavenly

Their design simple and petite

I find some are graciously pink

Most are paper white

They are quite beautiful to look at

It's their fragrance that captivates the mind

Nature did hold back

The gift bestowed on this tiny gem

Everyone should some day

Experience the beauty and mystique of

The Lily of the Valley

Just for You

Just one call is all it took

To make a mother smile

The tears I see and that lost look

Disappear for just a while

None but her will ever know

How great the pain inside

Nor the struggle it is not to show

All the feeling she must hide

If I could take and make it go

I would at the beat of a heart

But all I can do is let her know

I'm here at each day's start

If ever there is any doubt

How much one really cares

Look quietly deep into your heart

And know that I am there

Together Still

So many years have come and gone

Since the day you took my hand

When the two of us became as one

What a glorious day that was

I remember your hair

Your dress how it flowed

As you walked down the aisle to me

I could hear nothing but

The sound of your footsteps

I remember the look you had in your eyes

And the flowers you held in your hand

When you reached me

I touched you

At that moment it was only you and I

Just like now

My heart was yours

Long before the words

And the love has only grown deeper

It's good that we remember

But how could we forget

Something that so deeply

Changed our life

Gin Mill

The smell of liquor fills the air

The lonely traveler could be

A friend, a foe, or jokester

Only the chemist truly knows

He works with little direction

His mission is a simple one

Whether it's accomplished or not

Depends on time and chance

Many that stay really should not

But the chains on the stool hold fast

The smoke that drifts overhead

Makes its way to an open door

That signal tells me I should follow

I need to be somewhere else

If only that place held as hard as here

I could find my way out

Commander

When you stand alone at the end of the day

And take that moment just for you

Do you know what forces guide your way

Or is it just something you do

With each action taken there is an event

So many stand and protest

They do not realize the time that is spent

To believe in your heart you've done what is best

There are people and places that you'll never see

Even though with you pen you control

The destiny of some, the future of many

You've chosen your path, accepted your role

Most couldn't accomplish what you've had to do

There are many that wouldn't even try

So when it is over, I hope that for you

You never have to question why

Memorial Day

Glorious flags of red, white, and blue

Can be seen throughout the neighborhood

Children wave them in the streets

As the marching band plays on

Dignitaries and beauty queens

Pass by on classic convertibles

Some in the crown stand and wave

Some simply salute

As the VFW passes by

Some too old to march in cadence

But proud to walk with their comrades

When we think of hero or role model

Many ponder Ruth and Aaron

But the soldiers that pass you by

Paved the way

So today you can play catch with your children

The parade entertains those of all ages

But hopefully no one forgets

It's for the fallen, and those who've served

For those that are far from home on this day

We stand together and cross our hearts

For many a tear may fall

But the grateful patriot in us all

Should ask

Why not everyday

In this extraordinary time of political difference where factions of our society have, frankly, forgotten what sacrifices have been made over decades and continue to be made so that we can live and remain free is somewhat disturbing. The balance of power and those who control what society thinks has been misdirected over time by those who think they know better. Many of those have never had to make a sacrifice in order to convey what they deem patriotic. They choose to hide under the cloaks of those who have, knowing quite well that those who gave would not begrudge them their time to protest. Any person who has enjoyed the liberty and freedom of this great land and then chooses to assail it for the mere purpose of conforming to a group that they deem socially acceptable should be ashamed.